Rainbow Connections:

A Guide to Understanding and Supporting the LGBTQ+ Community

Contents

Rainbow Connections

Introduction

Welcome to our LGBTQ+ guide! Whether you are an LGBTQ+ individual, an ally, or simply curious about LGBTQ+ issues, we hope that this guide will serve as a valuable resource for you. The purpose of this guide is to provide accurate and inclusive information on a wide range of topics related to LGBTQ+ identity, health, relationships, legal rights, and advocacy. We believe that by providing this information, we can help support the well-being and empowerment of LGBTQ+ individuals and their allies.

As LGBTQ+ individuals and allies ourselves, we recognize the importance of creating safe and supportive spaces for LGBTQ+ people. We understand the struggles and the joys of living an authentic LGBTQ+ life, and we hope that this guide will help you navigate the complexities and nuances of LGBTQ+ identity and community.

This guide is designed to be accessible to readers of all backgrounds and levels of experience with LGBTQ+ issues. Whether you are just starting to explore your sexual or gender identity, navigating a difficult coming out process, or seeking resources for your health, relationships, or legal rights, this guide is here to help. We acknowledge that no guide can capture the full diversity and complexity of the LGBTQ+ community, and we encourage readers to seek out additional resources and perspectives as needed. However, we hope that this guide will provide a solid foundation for readers to understand and engage with LGBTQ+ issues.

Thank you for choosing to read this guide, and we hope that you find it helpful, informative, and empowering.

The purpose of this guide is to provide accurate and inclusive information on a wide range of topics related to LGBTQ+ identity, health, relationships, legal rights, and advocacy. We recognize that LGBTQ+ individuals and their allies may face unique challenges and experiences that can be difficult to navigate, and we believe that by providing this information, we can help support the well-being and empowerment of the LGBTQ+ community.

This guide is designed to be accessible to readers of all backgrounds and levels of experience with LGBTQ+ issues. Whether you are just starting to explore your sexual or gender identity, navigating a difficult coming out process, or seeking resources for your health, relationships, or legal rights, this guide is here to help.

We aim to provide comprehensive and trustworthy information on a variety of topics related to LGBTQ+ life, culture, and advocacy.

Some of the topics we will cover include:

- Sexual orientation and gender identity
- Coming out to family, friends, and colleagues
- Types of LGBTQ+ relationships, including dating and intimacy
- Mental and physical health issues affecting LGBTQ+ individuals

- Legal rights and protections for LGBTQ+ individuals
- Opportunities for advocacy and community building

By reading this guide, we hope that you will feel more informed, empowered, and connected to the larger LGBTQ+ community. We recognize that no guide can capture the full diversity and complexity of LGBTQ+ identity and culture, and we encourage readers to seek out additional resources and perspectives as needed. However, we believe that this guide will provide a solid foundation for readers to explore and engage with LGBTQ+ issues.

This guide covers a broad range of topics related to LGBTQ+ identity, health, relationships, legal rights, and advocacy. We aim to provide accurate and inclusive information that reflects the diverse experiences and perspectives of the LGBTQ+ community. However, we recognize that there are many diverse experiences and perspectives within the LGBTQ+ community, and we may not be able to address every question or concern that readers may have.

Some of the topics we will cover in this guide include:

- Understanding sexual orientation and gender identity
- Definitions and terminology
- Coming out and support for LGBTQ+ individuals and allies
- Relationships and Intimacy in the LGBTQ+ Community
- Types of LGBTQ+ relationships
- Maintaining healthy relationships
- Dating apps and websites for LGBTQ+ individuals
- Health and Wellness for the LGBTQ+ Community

- HIV/AIDS and other health issues affecting the LGBTQ+ community
- Finding inclusive healthcare providers and mental health resources
- Legal Rights and Protections for LGBTQ+ individuals
- Workplace discrimination and harassment
- Marriage equality and adoption rights
- Legal advocacy organizations and support resources
- Advocacy and Activism for the LGBTQ+ Community
- The history and progress of LGBTQ+ activism
- Opportunities for advocacy and community building
- Ways to get involved in advocacy efforts in your community

We also recognize that there may be topics and perspectives that are not covered in this guide. We encourage readers to seek out additional resources and perspectives as needed to gain a more comprehensive understanding of LGBTQ+ issues. Additionally, we recognize that language and terminology are constantly evolving within the LGBTQ+ community, and we have done our best to use inclusive and respectful language throughout this guide. However, we welcome feedback and suggestions for how we can improve and update this guide over time.

Our personal motivation for writing this guide comes from our experiences as LGBTQ+ individuals and allies. We have seen firsthand the importance of providing accurate and inclusive information to support the well-being and empowerment of the LGBTQ+ community. We have also experienced the struggles and joys of living an authentic LGBTQ+ life, and we believe that sharing our experiences and insights can help support others in their own journeys.

We recognize that there is a need for trustworthy and accessible resources on LGBTQ+ issues, particularly for individuals who may not have access to supportive communities or inclusive education. We hope that this guide can serve as a valuable resource for readers seeking to understand and engage with LGBTQ+ issues, regardless of their background or level of experience with LGBTQ+ topics.

Our goal in writing this guide is to provide accurate, comprehensive, and inclusive information on a variety of topics related to LGBTQ+ identity, health, relationships, legal rights, and advocacy. We believe that by providing this information, we can help support the well-being and empowerment of the LGBTQ+ community and its allies. We acknowledge that no guide can capture the full diversity and complexity of the LGBTQ+ community, and we encourage readers to seek out additional resources and perspectives as needed. However, we believe that this guide can provide a solid foundation for readers to explore and engage with LGBTQ+ issues. We welcome feedback and suggestions for how we can improve and update this guide over time, and we thank you for choosing to read it.

Chapter 1: LGBTQ+ Terms and Definitions

The LGBTQ+ community is diverse and complex, encompassing a wide range of identities and experiences. Understanding the terminology and definitions associated with LGBTQ+ identities is an essential step in becoming a supportive and inclusive ally. In this chapter, we will explore the most commonly used terms and definitions related to LGBTQ+ identities, as well as the importance of language and the evolution of LGBTQ+ terminology. By understanding and using inclusive language, we can create a more accepting and equitable society for all individuals, regardless of their sexual orientation or gender identity.

1.1 LGBTQ+ Terms and Definitions

Sexual Orientation

Heterosexual: Attracted to individuals of a different gender
Homosexual: Attracted to individuals of the same gender
Bisexual: Attracted to individuals of both the same and different genders
Pansexual: Attracted to individuals of any gender identity or expression
Asexual: Not sexually attracted to any gender

Gender Identity

Cisgender: Identifying with the gender assigned at birth
Transgender: Identifying with a gender other than the one assigned
at birth
Nonbinary: Identifying as neither male nor female
Genderqueer: Identifying with multiple gender identities or with a
fluid gender identity
Two-Spirit: A term used in some Indigenous cultures to describe
individuals who embody both masculine and feminine qualities

Pronouns

She/Her/Hers: Used to refer to someone who identifies as female
He/Him/His: Used to refer to someone who identifies as male
They/Them/Theirs: Used to refer to someone who identifies as
nonbinary or whose gender identity is unknown or undisclosed
Ze/Hir/Hirs: A set of gender-neutral pronouns that can be used in
place of she/her/hers or he/him/his
Xe/Xem/Xyr: Another set of gender-neutral pronouns that can be
used in place of she/her/hers or he/him/his

LGBTQ+ Terminology

Queer: An umbrella term used to describe individuals whose gender
identity or sexual orientation does not conform to societal norms

Intersex: Individuals who are born with biological sex characteristics that do not fit typical male or female classifications

Ally: A person who supports and advocates for the LGBTQ+ community

Out: Refers to a person who is openly LGBTQ+

Passing: Refers to an LGBTQ+ person who is able to "pass" as heterosexual or cisgender

Understanding LGBTQ+ terminology and language is an essential step in creating a more inclusive and supportive world for all individuals, regardless of their sexual orientation or gender identity. By familiarizing ourselves with these terms and symbols, we can better understand and appreciate the diversity within the LGBTQ+ community, and work towards creating a more accepting and equitable society.

Gender identity and expression are fundamental aspects of human identity. However, they can be complex and nuanced, and understanding them is essential for supporting and advocating for the LGBTQ+ community. In this chapter, we will explore gender identity and expression in depth, including the differences between gender identity and biological sex, the various gender identities and expressions within the LGBTQ+ community, and the ways in which individuals express their gender identities.

1.2 Gender Identity and Expression

Gender identity refers to a person's internal sense of their own gender, which may or may not align with the sex they were assigned at birth. Gender expression, on the other hand, refers to the way that a person expresses their gender identity to the world, through behaviors, clothing, and other means. Together, gender identity and expression are important components of a person's overall identity and sense of self.

For many people, their gender identity aligns with the sex they were assigned at birth. However, for some individuals, their gender identity is different from the sex they were assigned at birth. These individuals are often referred to as transgender or gender-nonconforming. Transgender people may identify as male, female, or nonbinary, meaning they don't identify exclusively as either male or female. Some transgender individuals may also choose to undergo medical interventions, such as hormone therapy or surgery, to alter their bodies to better align with their gender identity.

It is important to note that gender identity is not the same as sexual orientation. Sexual orientation refers to a person's emotional, romantic, or sexual attraction to other people, whereas gender identity is a person's internal sense of their own gender. Transgender individuals can have any sexual orientation, just like cisgender individuals.

Unfortunately, transgender individuals face significant discrimination and prejudice in many areas of society, including employment, housing, and healthcare. This discrimination can have a significant impact on their mental health and wellbeing. It is important for society as a whole to work towards greater acceptance and inclusion of transgender individuals, and to provide them with the same rights and opportunities as cisgender individuals.

In recent years, there has been increased awareness and acceptance of transgender individuals, thanks in part to the efforts of transgender activists and allies. This has led to increased visibility of transgender people in popular culture, as well as increased legal protections for transgender individuals. However, there is still much work to be done to ensure that transgender individuals are fully accepted and included in all areas of society.

In conclusion, gender identity and expression are important components of a person's overall identity and sense of self. For many people, their gender identity aligns with the sex they were assigned at birth, but for some individuals, their gender identity is different from their assigned sex. Transgender individuals face significant discrimination and prejudice, and it is important for society to work towards greater acceptance and inclusion of transgender individuals.

1.3 Sexual Orientation

Sexual orientation refers to a person's emotional, romantic, or sexual attraction to other people. It is a fundamental aspect of human identity, and can play a significant role in shaping a person's relationships and sense of self.

There are several different sexual orientations, including heterosexual (attraction to people of the opposite sex), homosexual (attraction to people of the same sex), bisexual (attraction to both men and women), and asexual (lack of sexual attraction to others). While sexual orientation is often thought of as a binary choice between heterosexual and homosexual, it is actually a spectrum, with many people falling somewhere in between.

Sexual orientation is a deeply personal aspect of identity, and can be influenced by a variety of factors, including biology, environment, and culture. While the exact causes of sexual orientation are not yet fully understood, research suggests that genetics, prenatal hormone exposure, and childhood experiences may all play a role.

Unfortunately, discrimination and prejudice against individuals based on their sexual orientation is still widespread in many parts of the world. LGBTQ+ individuals face significant barriers in areas such as employment, housing, healthcare, and education, and may also experience physical violence or harassment. This discrimination can have a profound impact on their mental health and wellbeing.

Efforts to combat discrimination and promote acceptance of LGBTQ+ individuals have been gaining momentum in recent years. Many countries have passed laws protecting the rights of LGBTQ+ individuals, and there has been a growing awareness and understanding of the diversity of sexual orientation and gender identity. However, there is still much work to be done to ensure that all individuals, regardless of sexual orientation or gender identity, are treated with respect and equality.

In conclusion, sexual orientation is a fundamental aspect of human identity, and can have a significant impact on a person's relationships and sense of self. While discrimination and prejudice against LGBTQ+ individuals still exists, efforts to promote acceptance and equality have been gaining momentum. It is important for society as a whole to work towards greater understanding and acceptance of the diversity of sexual orientation and gender identity, in order to create a more inclusive and just world for all.

1.4 Intersectionality

Intersectionality is a term coined by legal scholar and civil rights advocate Kimberlé Crenshaw in 1989. It refers to the complex ways in which different social identities, such as race, gender, class, sexuality, and ability, intersect and interact with one another, shaping a person's experiences and opportunities.

Intersectionality recognizes that individuals hold multiple identities simultaneously and that these identities are not separate from one another. Rather, they intersect and interact to create unique experiences of discrimination, privilege, and marginalization. For example, a woman of color may experience discrimination not only because of her gender but also because of her race, leading to a specific form of oppression that is different from that experienced by a white woman or a man of color.

Intersectionality emphasizes the importance of acknowledging and addressing the interconnectedness of different social identities in understanding and combatting discrimination and inequality. It highlights the ways in which systems of power and oppression are reinforced through the interaction of different social identities, and the need to address all forms of discrimination in order to create a more just and equitable society.

Intersectionality has been particularly influential in feminist and social justice movements, which have historically been dominated by white, middle-class women. By recognizing the experiences of marginalized communities, such as women of color, LGBTQ+ individuals, and people with disabilities, intersectionality has helped to broaden the scope of these movements and promote greater inclusivity and diversity.

However, intersectionality is not without its challenges. The complexity of intersecting social identities can make it difficult to address and fully understand the experiences of individuals who hold multiple marginalized identities. It can also be challenging to identify and address the ways in which privilege operates within and across different social identities.

In conclusion, intersectionality is a concept that emphasizes the complex ways in which different social identities intersect and interact with one another to shape a person's experiences and opportunities. It highlights the need to address all forms of discrimination and inequality in order to create a more just and equitable society. While challenging, intersectionality has the potential to promote greater inclusivity and diversity within feminist and social justice movements, and to create a more nuanced understanding of the experiences of marginalized communities.

Chapter 2: LGBTQ+ 101

Welcome to Chapter 2 of our LGBTQ+ guide. In this chapter, we will provide an overview of LGBTQ+ terminology, culture, and history to help readers gain a foundational understanding of LGBTQ+ identity and experiences. Whether you are new to LGBTQ+ topics or seeking a refresher, this chapter will provide a valuable foundation for engaging with the rest of the guide.

LGBTQ+ identity is complex and multifaceted, encompassing a wide range of sexual orientations, gender identities, and cultural expressions. Understanding and respecting this diversity is critical for building supportive and inclusive communities for LGBTQ+ individuals and their allies. This chapter aims to provide a broad overview of LGBTQ+ identity, history, and culture to help readers better understand and engage with LGBTQ+ issues.
We recognize that no single guide or chapter can capture the full complexity and diversity of LGBTQ+ identity and experiences. However, we hope that this chapter will serve as a starting point for readers seeking to understand and engage with LGBTQ+ issues. By the end of this chapter, we hope that readers will have a foundational understanding of LGBTQ+ terminology, culture, and history that will support their continued learning and engagement with the LGBTQ+ community.

We acknowledge that language and terminology are constantly evolving within the LGBTQ+ community, and we have done our best to use inclusive and respectful language throughout this guide. However, we welcome feedback and suggestions for how we can improve and update this chapter over time. Thank you for choosing to read this guide, and we hope that you find this chapter informative and engaging.

2.1 Sexual Orientation

Sexual orientation refers to an individual's enduring pattern of emotional, romantic, and/or sexual attractions to men, women, both genders, or no gender. Sexual orientation is often described using terms such as gay, lesbian, bisexual, pansexual, asexual, or straight. These terms can be useful in helping individuals communicate about their own sexual orientation and in creating community and support for people with shared experiences.

Definitions and Terminology: It's important to note that sexual orientation is not binary, meaning that it's not only about being attracted to men or women. Instead, there is a spectrum of sexual orientation that encompasses many different experiences and identities. Some of the terms used to describe sexual orientation include:

•	Gay: refers to individuals who are primarily attracted to people of the same gender as themselves.

•	Lesbian: refers to women who are primarily attracted to other women.

- Bisexual: refers to individuals who are attracted to people of both the same and different genders.
- Pansexual: refers to individuals who are attracted to people of all genders, or regardless of gender.
- Asexual: refers to individuals who experience little or no sexual attraction to others.
- Queer: can be used as an umbrella term to refer to individuals who identify as any non-heterosexual orientation or whose sexual orientation is more fluid or not easily categorized.

It's important to note that individuals may use different terms to describe their own sexual orientation or may prefer not to label their orientation at all. Additionally, sexual orientation can change over time or may be fluid, meaning that an individual's attractions may shift or evolve throughout their life.

History and Cultural Context: Sexual orientation has historically been a stigmatized and pathologized aspect of human experience. LGBTQ+ individuals have faced discrimination, violence, and oppression based on their sexual orientation. However, in recent decades, there has been significant progress in recognizing the rights and dignity of LGBTQ+ individuals, including marriage equality and other legal protections.

Today, many LGBTQ+ individuals and allies are working to create supportive and inclusive communities that respect and celebrate sexual orientation diversity. There are many resources and organizations available to support LGBTQ+ individuals and their allies, including community centers, support groups, and advocacy organizations. By the end of this subchapter, we hope that readers will have a deeper understanding of sexual orientation, including key definitions and terminology, and the historical and cultural context of sexual orientation diversity. We recognize that language and terminology are constantly evolving within the LGBTQ+ community, and we welcome feedback and suggestions for how we can improve and update this guide over time.

2.2 Gender Identity

Gender identity refers to an individual's internal sense of their own gender, which may or may not correspond to the sex they were assigned at birth. While gender is often thought of as a binary system (male or female), there is a growing understanding and recognition of gender diversity and non-binary identities.

Definitions and Terminology: Understanding gender identity requires an appreciation for the complexity and diversity of gender. Some of the terms used to describe gender identity include:

- Cisgender: refers to individuals who identify with the gender they were assigned at birth.
- Transgender: refers to individuals who identify with a gender that is different from the one they were assigned at birth.

- Non-binary: refers to individuals who identify with a gender that is not exclusively male or female, or who reject the gender binary altogether.
- Genderqueer: can be used as an umbrella term to describe individuals who identify as any gender identity that does not conform to the traditional binary model.
- Genderfluid: refers to individuals whose gender identity changes over time, or who feel that their gender identity is more fluid or not easily categorized.

It's important to note that individuals may use different terms to describe their own gender identity or may prefer not to label their gender identity at all. Additionally, gender identity is not determined by physical appearance or anatomy, but rather by an individual's internal sense of their own gender.

History and Cultural Context: The experiences of transgender and gender non-conforming individuals have varied widely throughout history and across cultures. While some cultures have recognized and respected gender diversity, others have stigmatized and pathologized it.

In recent decades, there has been growing awareness and recognition of transgender and non-binary identities. Many transgender and gender non-conforming individuals are working to create supportive and inclusive communities that respect and celebrate gender diversity. There are many resources and organizations available to support transgender and non-binary individuals and their allies, including community centers, support groups, and advocacy organizations.

By the end of this subchapter, we hope that readers will have a deeper understanding of gender identity, including key definitions and terminology, and the historical and cultural context of gender diversity. We recognize that language and terminology are constantly evolving within the LGBTQ+ community, and we welcome feedback and suggestions for how we can improve and update this guide over time.

2.3 Key Moments in LGBTQ+ History

The history of the LGBTQ+ rights movement is a rich and complex tapestry, woven together by the stories and experiences of countless individuals and communities. In this subchapter, we will explore some of the key moments in LGBTQ+ history that have shaped the modern LGBTQ+ rights movement.

Stonewall Riots: The Stonewall riots, which took place in New York City in 1969, are widely regarded as the spark that ignited the modern LGBTQ+ rights movement. In the early morning hours of June 28, police raided the Stonewall Inn, a popular gay bar in Greenwich Village. Instead of dispersing, as they had in previous raids, patrons and supporters of the bar fought back, sparking a multi-day riot that galvanized the LGBTQ+ community and led to increased activism and advocacy.

AIDS Epidemic: In the 1980s and 1990s, the AIDS epidemic had a profound impact on the LGBTQ+ community, particularly gay and bisexual men. Many individuals with AIDS faced discrimination, marginalization, and a lack of access to healthcare and support. However, the response to the epidemic also brought the LGBTQ+ community together and helped build networks of support and advocacy.

Marriage Equality: In recent decades, the fight for marriage equality has been a central issue in the LGBTQ+ rights movement. In 2015, the Supreme Court of the United States ruled that the Constitution guarantees the right to marry for same-sex couples, a landmark decision that represented a major victory for the LGBTQ+ community.

Legal Protections: While the fight for legal protections for LGBTQ+ individuals is far from over, there have been significant victories in recent decades. Many states and countries have passed laws protecting LGBTQ+ individuals from discrimination in employment, housing, and public accommodations. Additionally, many countries have recognized legal protections for transgender and non-binary individuals, including the right to change gender markers on legal documents.

By the end of this subchapter, we hope that readers will have a deeper appreciation for the key moments in LGBTQ+ history that have shaped the modern LGBTQ+ rights movement. We recognize that LGBTQ+ history is complex and multifaceted, and we encourage readers to seek out additional resources and perspectives to deepen their understanding of this important topic.

Conclusion: In this chapter, we provided an overview of LGBTQ+ terminology, culture, and history to help readers gain a foundational understanding of LGBTQ+ identity and experiences. We explored key concepts such as sexual orientation and gender identity, as well as important moments in LGBTQ+ history, such as the Stonewall riots and the fight for marriage equality.

It's important to remember that this chapter represents only a small slice of the vast and multifaceted world of LGBTQ+ identity and experiences. However, we hope that it has provided a useful foundation for readers seeking to understand and engage with LGBTQ+ issues. Understanding and respecting LGBTQ+ identity and experiences is critical for building inclusive and supportive communities for LGBTQ+ individuals and their allies.

As we move forward in this guide, we will continue to explore a wide range of topics related to LGBTQ+ identity, including health, relationships, legal rights, and advocacy. We recognize that language and terminology are constantly evolving within the LGBTQ+ community, and we have done our best to use inclusive and respectful language throughout this guide. However, we welcome feedback and suggestions for how we can improve and update this chapter and the rest of the guide over time.

Thank you for reading this chapter, and we hope that you will continue to engage with the rest of the guide.

Chapter 3: Coming Out

Welcome to Chapter 3 of our LGBTQ+ guide. In this chapter, we will explore the process of coming out as LGBTQ+ and provide resources and guidance for individuals considering coming out. We recognize that coming out is a deeply personal decision, and we aim to provide information and support that can help individuals navigate this important process.Coming out can be a powerful and transformative experience, but it can also be a challenging and emotional one. For many LGBTQ+ individuals, coming out is a critical step in developing a positive sense of self and building supportive relationships with friends, family, and community. However, the process of coming out can also be fraught with anxiety, fear, and uncertainty. In this chapter, we will explore the challenges and opportunities of coming out, as well as strategies for navigating this important process. We will discuss what coming out means, the impact it can have on an individual's life, and who to come out to and when. We will also explore some of the challenges that individuals may face when considering coming out, such as fear of rejection or discrimination, navigating family or cultural expectations, or dealing with internalized homophobia or transphobia.

Ultimately, our goal in this chapter is to provide information and support that can help individuals make informed decisions about coming out and build strong, healthy relationships with themselves and others. We recognize that coming out is a deeply personal decision, and we encourage individuals to seek out additional resources and support as needed. Thank you for choosing to read this guide, and we hope that you find this chapter informative and engaging.

3.1 Understanding Coming Out

Coming out refers to the process of disclosing one's LGBTQ+ identity to others. This can involve sharing one's sexual orientation, gender identity, or other aspects of one's LGBTQ+ identity with family, friends, coworkers, or others in one's life.

What is Coming Out?: Coming out means different things to different people, and there is no one "right" way to come out. For some individuals, coming out may involve sharing their LGBTQ+ identity with a trusted friend or family member. For others, it may involve making a public announcement or participating in LGBTQ+ activism. Ultimately, coming out is a personal decision that should be made on an individual basis.

The Impact of Coming Out: Coming out can have a profound impact on an individual's life, both positive and negative. For many individuals, coming out can be a powerful and transformative experience, helping them to develop a positive sense of self and build supportive relationships with others. However, coming out can also be a challenging and emotional experience, particularly if an individual faces rejection, discrimination, or other negative reactions.

Who to Come Out to and When: Deciding who to come out to and when can be a complex and personal decision. Some individuals may choose to come out to close friends and family first, while others may prefer to come out to a larger group or in a public setting. It's important to consider the potential risks and benefits of coming out to different people in one's life, and to seek out support and resources as needed.

By the end of this subchapter, we hope that readers will have a deeper understanding of what coming out means and the impact it can have on an individual's life. We recognize that coming out is a deeply personal decision, and we encourage individuals to seek out support and resources as they consider this important process.

3.2 Challenges of Coming Out

Coming out can be a difficult and emotional process, and many individuals face a variety of challenges and obstacles when considering coming out. In this subchapter, we will explore some of the common challenges that individuals may encounter when coming out as LGBTQ+.

Fear of Rejection or Discrimination: One of the most common challenges that individuals face when considering coming out is the fear of rejection or discrimination. LGBTQ+ individuals may worry that their loved ones or community will not accept them for who they are, or that they may face negative consequences, such as discrimination or violence, as a result of coming out.

Family and Cultural Expectations: Family and cultural expectations can also present a significant challenge for individuals considering coming out. Many LGBTQ+ individuals come from families or cultural backgrounds where LGBTQ+ identity is not accepted or understood, and may face pressure to conform to traditional gender and sexual norms.

Internalized Homophobia or Transphobia: Internalized homophobia or transphobia refers to negative attitudes or beliefs about one's own LGBTQ+ identity, which can make coming out more difficult. Internalized homophobia or transphobia may be the result of social stigma, discrimination, or personal beliefs and values.

By the end of this subchapter, we hope that readers will have a deeper understanding of some of the common challenges that individuals may face when considering coming out as LGBTQ+. It's important to remember that these challenges are normal and understandable, and that there are resources and support available to help individuals navigate the process of coming out. We encourage individuals to seek out support and resources as needed, and to take the time to make an informed decision about coming out that feels right for them.

In this chapter, we explored the process of coming out as LGBTQ+ and provided resources and guidance for individuals considering coming out. We discussed the challenges and opportunities of coming out, as well as strategies for navigating this important process.

Coming out is a deeply personal decision, and the decision to come out or not should be made on an individual basis. We recognize that coming out can be a complex and emotional process, and we encourage individuals to seek out support and resources as needed. By understanding what coming out means and the impact it can have on an individual's life, as well as the challenges that individuals may face when considering coming out, readers will be better equipped to navigate this important process. We hope that this chapter has provided useful information and support for individuals considering coming out, and we encourage readers to continue to explore the resources and support available to them as they move forward.

3.3 Strategies for Coming Out

Coming out is a deeply personal decision that can be challenging and emotional. However, there are strategies and resources available to help individuals navigate this important decision. In this subchapter, we will explore some of the key strategies for coming out and provide tips for individuals seeking support.

Building a Support System: Building a support system of friends, family, and other LGBTQ+ individuals can be an important part of coming out. A strong support system can provide emotional support, practical advice, and a sense of community for individuals who are coming out. Consider joining an LGBTQ+ support group or finding a therapist who specializes in LGBTQ+ issues.

Educating Loved Ones: Educating loved ones about LGBTQ+ issues can help them better understand and support the individual who is coming out. Providing information about LGBTQ+ identity, experiences, and terminology can be a helpful way to start the conversation. Consider sharing books, articles, or other resources with your loved ones.

Setting Boundaries and Managing Expectations: Setting boundaries and managing expectations can be an important part of the coming out process. This may involve setting clear boundaries with loved ones, such as what types of questions or behaviors are acceptable, and managing expectations around how loved ones may respond to the individual who is coming out. Consider setting aside time to talk to loved ones when you are ready, and prepare yourself for a range of reactions.

Resources and Support: There are a variety of resources and support available to individuals who are considering coming out. This may include online resources, support groups, or counseling services. It's important to seek out resources and support that are affirming and supportive of LGBTQ+ identity and experiences. Consider connecting with LGBTQ+ organizations in your area or finding a therapist who specializes in LGBTQ+ issues.

Tips:

- Take your time: There is no right or wrong timeline for coming out. Take the time you need to feel comfortable and prepared.

- Practice self-care: Coming out can be emotionally draining, so it's important to take care of yourself. Consider practicing self-care activities such as meditation, exercise, or spending time with friends.

- Consider safety: In some situations, coming out can be unsafe. Consider your safety and well-being before deciding to come out. It may be helpful to seek support from a trusted individual or organization.

- Be patient: It may take time for loved ones to process and accept your coming out. Be patient with them and give them space to ask questions and express their emotions.

By the end of this subchapter, we hope that readers will have a better understanding of the key strategies for coming out and the tips for seeking support. Remember, coming out is a deeply personal decision, and there is no one "right" way to come out. The most important thing is to do what feels right for you and to seek out support and resources as needed.

Chapter 4: Relationships

Introduction: Relationships can be a complex and challenging part of life, and this is especially true for individuals within the LGBTQ+ community. From navigating discrimination and societal expectations to building healthy, fulfilling connections with others, relationships can take many forms and present unique challenges for LGBTQ+ individuals.

In this chapter, we will explore relationships within the LGBTQ+ community and provide resources and guidance for building healthy, fulfilling connections with others. We will explore the unique dynamics and challenges of relationships within the LGBTQ+ community, and provide strategies and resources for building healthy relationships, navigating sex and intimacy, building families and parenting, and ending relationships.

We recognize that relationships can be a source of both joy and challenge for LGBTQ+ individuals, and our goal in this chapter is to provide information and support that can help individuals navigate the complexities of relationships and build strong, healthy connections with others. By the end of this chapter, we hope that readers will have a deeper understanding of relationships within the LGBTQ+ community, as well as strategies and resources for building healthy, fulfilling connections with others.

4.1 Understanding LGBTQ+ Relationships

Relationships within the LGBTQ+ community can take many forms, and can present unique challenges and opportunities for individuals. In this subchapter, we will explore the different types of relationships that exist within the LGBTQ+ community, as well as some of the challenges and opportunities of building and maintaining healthy relationships.

Types of LGBTQ+ Relationships: The LGBTQ+ community is a diverse and dynamic group of individuals, and relationships within this community can take many forms. Some common types of LGBTQ+ relationships include romantic relationships, friendships, chosen families, and more. These relationships may look different from traditional heterosexual relationships, and may be based on shared experiences and identities within the LGBTQ+ community.

Challenges of LGBTQ+ Relationships: While LGBTQ+ relationships can be a source of joy and fulfillment, they can also present unique challenges for individuals. Discrimination, heteronormativity, and societal expectations can all impact the dynamics of LGBTQ+ relationships, and individuals may face additional challenges based on their gender identity, sexual orientation, or other aspects of their identity.

Opportunities of LGBTQ+ Relationships: Despite these challenges, relationships within the LGBTQ+ community can also be a source of resilience and strength. Many LGBTQ+ individuals find community and support through their relationships, and may rely on their chosen families or other close connections to navigate challenges and celebrate successes.

By the end of this subchapter, we hope that readers will have a deeper understanding of the unique dynamics and challenges of relationships within the LGBTQ+ community. Remember, relationships can take many forms and can be a source of both joy and challenge for LGBTQ+ individuals. We encourage individuals to seek out support and resources as they navigate relationships and to prioritize their own well-being and happiness.

4.2 Building Healthy Relationships

Building healthy and fulfilling relationships is important for all individuals, and this is especially true for those within the LGBTQ+ community. In this subchapter, we will explore some strategies for building healthy relationships, and discuss some of the key aspects of healthy relationships.

Communication: Communication is a crucial aspect of any healthy relationship, and this is especially true for LGBTQ+ individuals who may be navigating unique challenges and dynamics. Communication can help individuals build trust, set boundaries, and navigate challenges within relationships. Some key skills for effective communication include active listening, using "I" statements, and being open to feedback.

Boundaries: Setting boundaries is an important part of building healthy relationships. This may involve setting boundaries around communication, physical touch, or other aspects of the relationship. It's important for individuals to communicate their boundaries clearly, and to respect the boundaries of their partner or friend.

Trust and Respect: Trust and respect are essential aspects of any healthy relationship. These qualities can be especially important for LGBTQ+ individuals who may be navigating societal discrimination or other challenges. Building trust and respect can involve showing vulnerability, being consistent, and being supportive of each other's growth and development.

Navigating Challenges: Challenges are a natural part of any relationship, and this is especially true for relationships within the LGBTQ+ community. Navigating challenges may involve conflict resolution, finding common ground, or seeking out support from friends or loved ones. It's important for individuals to approach challenges with a growth mindset and a willingness to learn and adapt.

By the end of this subchapter, we hope that readers will have a deeper understanding of the key aspects of healthy relationships, and some strategies for building healthy and fulfilling connections with others. Remember, building healthy relationships takes time and effort, but can be a source of joy and growth for individuals within the LGBTQ+ community. We encourage individuals to seek out support and resources as they navigate relationships and to prioritize their own well-being and happiness.

4.3 Navigating Sex and Intimacy

Sex and intimacy are important aspects of many relationships, and this is no different for individuals within the LGBTQ+ community. In this subchapter, we will explore some of the key aspects of sex and intimacy within LGBTQ+ relationships, and provide resources and guidance for staying safe and healthy when engaging in sexual activity.

Types of Sexual and Romantic Attraction: Individuals within the LGBTQ+ community may experience a wide range of sexual and romantic attraction. This may include attraction to the same gender, multiple genders, or no gender at all. Understanding and exploring one's own sexual and romantic attraction can be an important part of building healthy relationships.

Consent and Communication: Consent and communication are essential aspects of any healthy sexual or intimate relationship. This may involve discussing boundaries, preferences, and expectations with one's partner or partners, and seeking consent before engaging in sexual activity. It's important for individuals to prioritize their own comfort and safety, and to respect the boundaries of their partner or partners.

Staying Safe and Healthy: Staying safe and healthy when engaging in sexual activity is crucial for all individuals, and this is especially true for individuals within the LGBTQ+ community who may be at increased risk for certain health concerns. It's important for individuals to practice safe sex, get regular STI screenings, and to seek out resources and support as needed.

Resources and Support: There are a variety of resources and support available to individuals within the LGBTQ+ community who are navigating sex and intimacy. This may include online resources, support groups, or counseling services. It's important for individuals to seek out resources and support that are affirming and supportive of LGBTQ+ identity and experiences.

By the end of this subchapter, we hope that readers will have a deeper understanding of the different aspects of sex and intimacy within LGBTQ+ relationships, as well as strategies and resources for staying safe and healthy when engaging in sexual activity. Remember, sexual and intimate relationships can be a source of joy and connection, but it's important to prioritize one's own comfort and safety. We encourage individuals to seek out support and resources as needed.

4.4 Family and Parenting

Building families and parenting can be a complex and challenging part of life for anyone, and this is especially true for individuals within the LGBTQ+ community. In this subchapter, we will explore the unique challenges and opportunities of building families and parenting within the LGBTQ+ community, and provide resources and guidance for building healthy, supportive family relationships. Types of Families: Families within the LGBTQ+ community can take many different forms, and may include chosen families, families of origin, and more. These families may look different from traditional heterosexual families, and may involve a range of different structures and dynamics.

Legal and Social Barriers: Despite recent progress towards LGBTQ+ rights, there are still legal and social barriers that may impact the ability of LGBTQ+ individuals to build families or parent. These barriers may include restrictions on adoption and surrogacy, discrimination from healthcare providers or other professionals, and more.

Building Healthy Families: Building healthy, supportive family relationships is crucial for all individuals, and this is no different for individuals within the LGBTQ+ community. Some key strategies for building healthy family relationships may include open communication, setting boundaries, and seeking out support from friends or professionals when needed.

Parenting: Parenting within the LGBTQ+ community can present unique challenges and opportunities. It's important for individuals to prioritize their own well-being and the well-being of their children, and to seek out resources and support as needed. Some key resources for LGBTQ+ parents may include parenting groups, counseling services, and more.

By the end of this subchapter, we hope that readers will have a deeper understanding of the unique challenges and opportunities of building families and parenting within the LGBTQ+ community, as well as strategies and resources for building healthy, supportive family relationships. Remember, building healthy family relationships can take time and effort, but can be a source of joy and growth for individuals within the LGBTQ+ community. We encourage individuals to seek out support and resources as needed.

4.5 Ending Relationships

Ending a relationship can be a difficult and emotional process for anyone, and this is no different for individuals within the LGBTQ+ community. In this subchapter, we will explore some of the reasons why relationships may end, and provide guidance and support for navigating the emotional and practical aspects of ending a relationship.

Reasons for Ending Relationships: Relationships within the LGBTQ+ community may end for a variety of different reasons. Some common reasons for ending relationships may include changes in life circumstances, growing apart, or differing expectations or goals. It's important for individuals to reflect on their own reasons for ending a relationship, and to communicate these reasons clearly and respectfully to their partner or partners.

Emotional Aspects of Ending Relationships: Ending a relationship can be an emotional and challenging process. It's important for individuals to prioritize their own well-being and to seek out support from friends or professionals as needed. Some common emotions that may arise during the process of ending a relationship may include sadness, anger, or uncertainty.

Practical Aspects of Ending Relationships: Ending a relationship can also involve a number of practical considerations, such as dividing assets or living arrangements. It's important for individuals to approach these practical considerations with a sense of fairness and respect, and to seek out legal or professional support as needed.

Moving Forward: Ending a relationship can be a difficult and painful process, but it can also be an opportunity for growth and self-reflection. It's important for individuals to take the time they need to process their emotions and to reflect on what they have learned from the relationship. Moving forward may involve seeking out new connections and opportunities, and taking time to prioritize one's own well-being and happiness.

By the end of this subchapter, we hope that readers will have a deeper understanding of the emotional and practical aspects of ending relationships within the LGBTQ+ community, as well as strategies and resources for moving forward and building healthy, fulfilling connections with others. Remember, ending a relationship can be a painful and challenging process, but it can also be an opportunity for growth and self-reflection. We encourage individuals to seek out support and resources as needed.

Relationships can be a complex and challenging part of life, and this is especially true for individuals within the LGBTQ+ community. In this chapter, we have explored the unique dynamics and challenges of relationships within the LGBTQ+ community, and provided resources and guidance for building healthy, fulfilling connections with others.

We have explored the different types of relationships that exist within the LGBTQ+ community, and some of the challenges and opportunities of building and maintaining healthy relationships. We have discussed some key aspects of healthy relationships, such as communication, boundaries, trust and respect, and navigating challenges.

We have also explored some of the key aspects of sex and intimacy within LGBTQ+ relationships, and provided resources and guidance for staying safe and healthy when engaging in sexual activity. Additionally, we have discussed the unique challenges and opportunities of building families and parenting within the LGBTQ+ community, and provided guidance and support for navigating the emotional and practical aspects of ending a relationship.

Remember, building healthy relationships takes time and effort, but can be a source of joy and growth for individuals within the LGBTQ+ community. We encourage individuals to seek out support and resources as they navigate relationships, and to prioritize their own well-being and happiness.

By the end of this chapter, we hope that readers will have a deeper understanding of relationships within the LGBTQ+ community, as well as strategies and resources for building healthy, fulfilling connections with others. We encourage individuals to continue to seek out support and resources as they navigate relationships, and to prioritize their own well-being and happiness.

Chapter 5: Health and Wellness

Individuals within the LGBTQ+ community face a range of unique health and wellness concerns, ranging from physical health concerns such as HIV/AIDS and STIs to mental health concerns such as anxiety and depression. Additionally, discrimination, social stigma, and legal barriers can create additional challenges when it comes to accessing healthcare and support.

In this chapter, we will explore some of the key aspects of health and wellness within the LGBTQ+ community, and provide resources and guidance for staying healthy and well. We will discuss some of the unique health concerns facing LGBTQ+ individuals, and provide guidance and resources for seeking out support and treatment. Remember, prioritizing your own health and wellness is essential for building a fulfilling and happy life. We encourage individuals within the LGBTQ+ community to seek out support and resources as needed, and to prioritize their own well-being and happiness. By the end of this chapter, we hope that readers will have a deeper understanding of the unique health and wellness concerns facing individuals within the LGBTQ+ community, and the resources and strategies for staying healthy and well.

5.1 Mental Health and Wellness

Mental health is an important aspect of overall health and wellness for all individuals, and this is no different for individuals within the LGBTQ+ community. In this subchapter, we will explore some of the unique mental health concerns facing LGBTQ+ individuals, and provide resources and guidance for staying mentally and emotionally healthy.

Some common mental health concerns facing individuals within the LGBTQ+ community may include anxiety, depression, and trauma. These concerns may be related to experiences of discrimination, social stigma, or violence. It's important for individuals to seek out support and resources as needed, and to prioritize their own well-being and self-care.

There are a range of resources and support available to individuals within the LGBTQ+ community who are experiencing mental health concerns. This may include counseling services, support groups, or online resources. It's important for individuals to seek out resources and support that are affirming and supportive of LGBTQ+ identity and experiences.

Additionally, building healthy coping strategies and self-care routines can be an important part of staying mentally and emotionally healthy. Some key self-care strategies for mental health may include mindfulness, exercise, and spending time with supportive friends and family.

By the end of this subchapter, we hope that readers will have a deeper understanding of the unique mental health concerns facing individuals within the LGBTQ+ community, as well as strategies and resources for staying mentally and emotionally healthy. Remember, prioritizing your own mental health and well-being is essential for building a fulfilling and happy life. We encourage individuals to seek out support and resources as needed, and to prioritize their own well-being and happiness.

5.2 Physical Health and Wellness

Physical health is an important aspect of overall health and wellness for all individuals, and this is no different for individuals within the LGBTQ+ community. In this subchapter, we will explore some of the unique physical health concerns facing LGBTQ+ individuals, and provide resources and guidance for staying physically healthy. Some common physical health concerns facing individuals within the LGBTQ+ community may include HIV/AIDS, STIs, and cancer. These concerns may be related to a range of factors, including discrimination, social stigma, or lack of access to healthcare.
It's important for individuals within the LGBTQ+ community to prioritize their physical health and well-being, and to seek out support and resources as needed. This may include regular check-ups with a healthcare provider, as well as staying informed about health risks and strategies for reducing risk.

There are a range of resources and support available to individuals within the LGBTQ+ community who are experiencing physical health concerns. This may include healthcare providers who are trained to provide affirming and supportive care to LGBTQ+ individuals, as well as support groups or online resources.

In addition to seeking out support and resources, building healthy habits and self-care routines can be an important part of staying physically healthy. Some key strategies for physical health may include regular exercise, healthy nutrition, and practicing safe sex. By the end of this subchapter, we hope that readers will have a deeper understanding of the unique physical health concerns facing individuals within the LGBTQ+ community, as well as strategies and resources for staying physically healthy. Remember, prioritizing your own physical health and well-being is essential for building a fulfilling and happy life. We encourage individuals to seek out support and resources as needed, and to prioritize their own well-being and happiness.

5.3 Substance Use and Addiction

Substance use and addiction can be a concern for individuals within any community, and this is no different for individuals within the LGBTQ+ community. In this subchapter, we will explore some of the unique concerns around substance use and addiction within the LGBTQ+ community, and provide guidance and resources for seeking out support and treatment.

By the end of this subchapter, we hope that readers will have a deeper understanding of the unique challenges facing individuals within the LGBTQ+ community when it comes to accessing healthcare, as well as resources and strategies for finding affirming and supportive healthcare providers. Remember, access to healthcare is a fundamental right for all individuals, and individuals within the LGBTQ+ community should not face discrimination or barriers when seeking out care. We encourage individuals to seek out support and resources as needed, and to prioritize their own well-being and happiness.

5.5 Self-Care and Wellness Strategies

Prioritizing self-care and wellness strategies is an important part of overall health and well-being for individuals within the LGBTQ+ community. In this subchapter, we will explore some of the key strategies for staying healthy and well through self-care and wellness practices.

Self-care can take many different forms, and it's important for individuals to find the self-care practices that work best for them. Some common self-care strategies may include mindfulness, meditation, exercise, or spending time in nature. It's important to prioritize regular self-care routines as a way of building resilience and coping with stress.

Additionally, there are a range of wellness practices that can be beneficial for individuals within the LGBTQ+ community. This may include practices such as yoga, acupuncture, or massage therapy. These practices can be beneficial for both physical and mental health, and can help to reduce stress and promote overall well-being. It's important for individuals within the LGBTQ+ community to prioritize their own self-care and wellness, and to seek out resources and support as needed. This may include attending support groups or workshops, seeking out resources online, or finding a mental health or wellness practitioner who is trained to provide affirming and supportive care.

By the end of this subchapter, we hope that readers will have a deeper understanding of the importance of self-care and wellness practices for overall health and well-being, as well as strategies and resources for incorporating these practices into their daily lives. Remember, prioritizing self-care and wellness is essential for building a fulfilling and happy life. We encourage individuals to seek out support and resources as needed, and to prioritize their own well-being and happiness.

In this chapter, we have explored some of the unique health and wellness concerns facing individuals within the LGBTQ+ community, and provided resources and guidance for staying healthy and well. From mental health and wellness, to physical health and wellness, to substance use and addiction, we have discussed a range of important topics and strategies for staying healthy and well.

Remember, prioritizing your own health and wellness is essential for building a fulfilling and happy life. We encourage individuals within the LGBTQ+ community to seek out support and resources as needed, and to prioritize their own well-being and happiness. By incorporating the strategies and resources discussed in this chapter into your daily life, you can build resilience, cope with stress, and promote overall health and well-being.

We hope that this chapter has provided readers with a deeper understanding of the unique health and wellness concerns facing individuals within the LGBTQ+ community, as well as strategies and resources for staying healthy and well. Remember, support and resources are available to you, and you do not have to face these challenges alone. We encourage you to prioritize your own health and wellness, and to seek out support and resources as needed.

Chapter 6: Legal Rights

Legal rights are an essential aspect of the well-being of all individuals, and this is no different for individuals within the LGBTQ+ community. Accessing legal rights and protections can be a critical part of building a safe and fulfilling life for LGBTQ+ individuals, and can help to ensure that discrimination and violence are addressed appropriately.

In this chapter, we will explore some of the key legal rights and protections available to individuals within the LGBTQ+ community, and provide resources and guidance for understanding and accessing these rights. From marriage and family rights, to employment and workplace protections, to housing and public accommodation protections, we will discuss a range of important topics and strategies for accessing legal rights and protections.

Remember, knowledge is power when it comes to understanding and accessing legal rights and protections. We encourage individuals within the LGBTQ+ community to seek out legal support and resources as needed, and to prioritize their own safety and well-being. By advocating for your own rights and understanding the legal system, you can build resilience and protect your own well-being. Let's dive in!

6.1: Marriage and Family Rights

The legal recognition of marriage and family rights has been a key issue for individuals within the LGBTQ+ community. While significant progress has been made in recent years, access to legal rights and protections related to marriage and family can still be a challenge for some individuals.

In this subchapter, we will explore the legal rights and protections available to individuals within the LGBTQ+ community when it comes to marriage and family rights. This may include discussing the legal history of marriage equality, as well as providing guidance and resources for navigating the legal system when it comes to adoption, surrogacy, and other family-related legal concerns. Marriage Equality: In 2015, the United States Supreme Court ruled in favor of marriage equality in the landmark case Obergefell v. Hodges. This decision effectively legalized same-sex marriage across the United States, granting LGBTQ+ individuals the same legal rights and protections as heterosexual couples. However, despite this legal victory, same-sex couples may still face discrimination or challenges in accessing legal marriage rights, particularly in areas with more conservative or discriminatory social attitudes.

Adoption and Surrogacy: For LGBTQ+ individuals who wish to start a family through adoption or surrogacy, there are a range of legal considerations to keep in mind. While legal protections have been put in place to prevent discrimination against LGBTQ+ individuals in adoption and surrogacy processes, challenges and obstacles can still arise. It is important for individuals to seek out legal support and resources when navigating these processes, and to be aware of their legal rights and protections throughout.

By the end of this subchapter, we hope that readers will have a deeper understanding of the legal rights and protections available to individuals within the LGBTQ+ community when it comes to marriage and family rights. Remember, accessing legal rights and protections is an essential aspect of building a safe and fulfilling life for LGBTQ+ individuals. We encourage individuals to seek out legal support and resources as needed, and to prioritize their own safety and well-being.

6.2: Employment and Workplace Protections

Access to employment and workplace protections is an important issue for individuals within the LGBTQ+ community. Historically, discrimination against LGBTQ+ individuals in the workplace has been common, but there have been significant strides made in recent years to address these issues and protect the rights of LGBTQ+ workers.

Legal Protections: In recent years, legal protections have been put in place to prevent discrimination against LGBTQ+ individuals in the workplace. For example, Title VII of the Civil Rights Act of 1964, which prohibits employment discrimination based on sex, has been interpreted by some courts to include sexual orientation and gender identity as protected classes. Additionally, many states and local jurisdictions have passed their own anti-discrimination laws that explicitly protect LGBTQ+ individuals in the workplace.

Navigating Workplace Discrimination: Despite legal protections, workplace discrimination against LGBTQ+ individuals can still occur. Discrimination may take the form of harassment, unequal pay, or wrongful termination, among other things. It is important for individuals to be aware of their legal rights and protections, and to seek out legal support and resources when necessary.

Filing Complaints: Individuals who experience discrimination in the workplace may file a complaint with the Equal Employment Opportunity Commission (EEOC), a federal agency that is responsible for enforcing civil rights laws related to employment. The EEOC investigates complaints and can take action against employers who are found to have violated anti-discrimination laws. It is important to note that there are specific deadlines for filing complaints with the EEOC, and that legal support and representation may be helpful in navigating the process.

Working with Legal Professionals: Working with legal professionals who are trained to provide support and representation in cases of discrimination can be a valuable resource for individuals within the LGBTQ+ community. This may include lawyers who specialize in employment law, as well as advocacy organizations that provide legal support and resources. Seeking out legal support and representation can help to ensure that individuals' legal rights and protections are upheld, and can help to prevent discrimination from occurring in the future.

By the end of this subchapter, we hope that readers will have a deeper understanding of the legal protections available to individuals within the LGBTQ+ community when it comes to employment and workplace rights, as well as strategies and resources for navigating workplace discrimination. Remember, access to employment and workplace protections is an essential aspect of building a fulfilling and successful life for LGBTQ+ individuals. We encourage individuals to seek out legal support and resources as needed, and to prioritize their own safety and well-being.

6.3: Housing and Public Accommodation Protections

Access to safe and affordable housing and public accommodations is an essential aspect of the well-being of individuals within the LGBTQ+ community. Historically, discrimination against LGBTQ+ individuals in housing and public spaces has been common, but there have been significant strides made in recent years to address these issues and protect the rights of LGBTQ+ individuals.

In this subchapter, we will explore the legal protections available to individuals within the LGBTQ+ community when it comes to housing and public accommodation rights. This may include discussing the legal history of discrimination against LGBTQ+ individuals in housing and public spaces, as well as providing guidance and resources for navigating discrimination and seeking legal support.

Legal Protections: There are a range of legal protections in place to prevent discrimination against LGBTQ+ individuals in housing and public accommodations. For example, the Fair Housing Act prohibits discrimination based on race, color, religion, national origin, sex, familial status, and disability, and has been interpreted by some courts to include sexual orientation and gender identity as protected classes. Additionally, many states and local jurisdictions have passed their own anti-discrimination laws that explicitly protect LGBTQ+ individuals in housing and public accommodations.

Navigating Discrimination: Despite legal protections, discrimination against LGBTQ+ individuals in housing and public accommodations can still occur. Discrimination may take the form of denial of housing, harassment, or refusal of service in public accommodations. It is important for individuals to be aware of their legal rights and protections, and to seek out legal support and resources when necessary.

Filing Complaints: Individuals who experience discrimination in housing or public accommodations may file a complaint with the appropriate state or local agency that is responsible for enforcing anti-discrimination laws. It is important to note that there are specific deadlines for filing complaints, and that legal support and representation may be helpful in navigating the process.

Working with Legal Professionals: Working with legal professionals who are trained to provide support and representation in cases of discrimination can be a valuable resource for individuals within the LGBTQ+ community. This may include lawyers who specialize in housing law or public accommodations law, as well as advocacy organizations that provide legal support and resources. Seeking out legal support and representation can help to ensure that individuals' legal rights and protections are upheld, and can help to prevent discrimination from occurring in the future.

By the end of this subchapter, we hope that readers will have a deeper understanding of the legal protections available to individuals within the LGBTQ+ community when it comes to housing and public accommodation rights, as well as strategies and resources for navigating discrimination. Remember, access to safe and affordable housing and public accommodations is an essential aspect of building a safe and fulfilling life for LGBTQ+ individuals. We encourage individuals to seek out legal support and resources as needed, and to prioritize their own safety and well-being.

6.4: Health Care and Insurance Protections

Access to health care and insurance protections is a critical issue for individuals within the LGBTQ+ community. Discrimination and lack of access to health care services can have serious consequences for individuals' well-being, and can create significant barriers to receiving the care and treatment that is necessary for a healthy and fulfilling life.

In this subchapter, we will explore the legal protections available to individuals within the LGBTQ+ community when it comes to health care and insurance rights. This may include discussing the history of discrimination against LGBTQ+ individuals in health care settings, as well as providing guidance and resources for navigating discrimination and seeking legal support.

Legal Protections: There are a range of legal protections in place to prevent discrimination against LGBTQ+ individuals in health care and insurance settings. For example, the Affordable Care Act (ACA) includes provisions that prohibit discrimination based on sex, which has been interpreted by some courts to include sexual orientation and gender identity as protected classes. Additionally, many states and local jurisdictions have passed their own anti-discrimination laws that explicitly protect LGBTQ+ individuals in health care settings.

Navigating Discrimination: Despite legal protections, discrimination against LGBTQ+ individuals in health care and insurance settings can still occur. Discrimination may take the form of denial of care, harassment, or unequal access to insurance benefits. It is important for individuals to be aware of their legal rights and protections, and to seek out legal support and resources when necessary.

Filing Complaints: Individuals who experience discrimination in health care or insurance settings may file a complaint with the appropriate state or federal agency that is responsible for enforcing anti-discrimination laws. It is important to note that there are specific deadlines for filing complaints, and that legal support and representation may be helpful in navigating the process.

Working with Legal Professionals: Working with legal professionals who are trained to provide support and representation in cases of discrimination can be a valuable resource for individuals within the LGBTQ+ community. This may include lawyers who specialize in health care law or insurance law, as well as advocacy organizations that provide legal support and resources. Seeking out legal support and representation can help to ensure that individuals' legal rights and protections are upheld, and can help to prevent discrimination from occurring in the future.

By the end of this subchapter, we hope that readers will have a deeper understanding of the legal protections available to individuals within the LGBTQ+ community when it comes to health care and insurance rights, as well as strategies and resources for navigating discrimination. Remember, access to health care and insurance protections is an essential aspect of building a safe and fulfilling life for LGBTQ+ individuals. We encourage individuals to seek out legal support and resources as needed, and to prioritize their own safety and well-being.

In conclusion, Chapter 6 has examined the legal rights and protections available to individuals within the LGBTQ+ community. We have discussed the progress that has been made in recent years to address discrimination and protect the rights of LGBTQ+ individuals in a range of areas, including employment, housing, public accommodations, health care, and insurance.

It is important for individuals within the LGBTQ+ community to be aware of their legal rights and to seek out legal support and representation when necessary. Navigating discrimination can be challenging, but by working with legal professionals and advocacy organizations, individuals can better protect themselves and ensure that their legal rights are upheld.

We encourage individuals to be proactive in seeking out legal support and resources, and to prioritize their own safety and well-being. With continued advocacy and support, we can work towards a future where all individuals are able to access their legal rights and live full and meaningful lives.

In the next chapter, we will explore strategies and resources for building supportive and inclusive communities for LGBTQ+ individuals. By working together to create safe and welcoming spaces, we can help to support and empower individuals within the LGBTQ+ community, and create a more just and equitable world for all.

Chapter 7: Activism and Advocacy

Introduction: Chapter 7 explores strategies and resources for individuals within the LGBTQ+ community who want to get involved in activism and advocacy. Activism and advocacy have played a critical role in promoting LGBTQ+ rights and creating social change, and have been instrumental in securing legal protections, public recognition, and cultural acceptance for the LGBTQ+ community. In this chapter, we will explore why activism and advocacy are important, how to get involved, and strategies for making a meaningful impact. We will also provide resources for individuals who want to get involved in activism and advocacy, and explore the future of LGBTQ+ activism and advocacy. By getting involved in activism and advocacy, individuals within the LGBTQ+ community can make a meaningful impact and work towards a more just and equitable world for all.

7.1: Why Activism and Advocacy are Important

Activism and advocacy have played a critical role in promoting LGBTQ+ rights and creating social change. From the Stonewall riots to the fight for marriage equality, activism and advocacy have been instrumental in securing legal protections, public recognition, and cultural acceptance for the LGBTQ+ community.

The importance of activism and advocacy extends beyond legal and political victories, however. Activism and advocacy can also play a critical role in fostering a sense of community and belonging among LGBTQ+ individuals, and can create opportunities for individuals to connect with others who share similar experiences and perspectives. Activism and advocacy also serve as a way for LGBTQ+ individuals to claim their space and demand recognition, visibility, and respect. By speaking out, organizing, and taking action, individuals can work to challenge stereotypes, combat discrimination, and push for social change.

Finally, activism and advocacy can be a way for individuals to make a meaningful impact on the world around them. Whether through grassroots organizing, direct action, or policy advocacy, individuals within the LGBTQ+ community can use their voices and their actions to create change and promote equality and justice for all. By understanding the importance of activism and advocacy in promoting LGBTQ+ rights and creating social change, individuals can be inspired to get involved and make a difference in their communities and beyond. In the next subchapter, we will explore strategies for getting involved in activism and advocacy as an LGBTQ+ individual.

7.2: Getting Involved in Activism and Advocacy

Getting involved in activism and advocacy can be a meaningful and empowering way for LGBTQ+ individuals to make a difference in their communities and beyond. Whether through grassroots organizing, direct action, or policy advocacy, there are a variety of ways to get involved in activism and advocacy as an LGBTQ+ individual.

One of the first steps in getting involved in activism and advocacy is to identify the issues and causes that matter most to you. This may involve exploring different areas of LGBTQ+ activism, such as promoting legal protections, fighting for transgender rights, or advocating for LGBTQ+ youth. By identifying the issues that resonate with you, you can focus your efforts and make a meaningful impact.

Once you have identified the issues and causes that matter most to you, you can begin to explore different types of activism and advocacy. This may include grassroots organizing, which involves working with other individuals and organizations to build momentum and create change from the ground up. Direct action, such as protests and civil disobedience, can also be an effective way to draw attention to issues and generate momentum for change. Policy advocacy involves working with lawmakers and other decision-makers to shape policies and laws that impact the LGBTQ+ community.

To get involved in activism and advocacy, you may consider reaching out to local organizations or groups that are working on issues that you care about. This may involve attending meetings and events, volunteering your time and resources, and building connections with other activists and advocates.

Finally, it is important to prioritize your own well-being and self-care as you engage in activism and advocacy. This may involve setting boundaries, seeking support from others, and taking breaks as needed to avoid burnout and fatigue.

By exploring different types of activism and advocacy and finding the issues that resonate with you, you can make a meaningful impact and work towards a more just and equitable world for all. In the next subchapter, we will explore strategies for making an impact as an LGBTQ+ activist or advocate.

7.3: Strategies for Making an Impact

Making a meaningful impact as an LGBTQ+ activist or advocate involves understanding the issues, building connections with others, and creating effective campaigns and initiatives. Here are some strategies for making an impact as an LGBTQ+ activist or advocate:

1.   Community Engagement: Community engagement is an important part of promoting LGBTQ+ rights and creating social change. This may involve creating and participating in community events and initiatives, reaching out to marginalized groups within the LGBTQ+ community, and engaging with other local organizations and advocacy groups.

2.	Education and Awareness: Education and awareness are important components of creating social change. This may involve creating and sharing educational materials, hosting workshops and presentations, and engaging with individuals who may not be familiar with LGBTQ+ issues.

3.	Effective Campaigns: Effective campaigns are essential for creating change. This may involve creating petitions, building online campaigns, and creating effective messaging and branding to promote the campaign.

4.	Policy Advocacy: Policy advocacy involves working with lawmakers and other decision-makers to shape policies and laws that impact the LGBTQ+ community. This may involve meeting with elected officials, organizing rallies, and working with other advocacy groups to create change.

5.	Self-Care and Burnout Prevention: It is important to prioritize your own well-being and self-care as you engage in activism and advocacy. This may involve setting boundaries, seeking support from others, and taking breaks as needed to avoid burnout and fatigue.

By utilizing these strategies and finding ways to make a meaningful impact, individuals within the LGBTQ+ community can work towards a more just and equitable world for all. In the next subchapter, we will explore resources for individuals who want to get involved in activism and advocacy.

7.4: Resources for Activism and Advocacy

There are a variety of resources available for individuals within the LGBTQ+ community who want to get involved in activism and advocacy. Here are some resources that may be helpful:

1.   LGBTQ+ Organizations: There are a variety of LGBTQ+ organizations and advocacy groups that focus on different issues and causes. Some examples of LGBTQ+ organizations include GLAAD, Human Rights Campaign, and the Trevor Project.

2.   Directories: Directories and online resources can be helpful for identifying organizations and groups that are working on specific issues or causes. Some directories for LGBTQ+ organizations include the National LGBTQ Task Force's directory and the Gay & Lesbian Alliance Against Defamation (GLAAD) directory.

3.   Toolkits and Guides: There are a variety of toolkits and guides available for individuals who want to get involved in activism and advocacy. These may provide tips and strategies for effective campaigning, guidance on building community and connections, and resources for avoiding burnout and fatigue.

4.   Events and Conferences: Attending events and conferences can be a helpful way to learn about LGBTQ+ issues, connect with other activists and advocates, and explore different strategies for creating change.

5.   Social Media and Online Communities: Social media and online communities can be a helpful way to connect with other LGBTQ+ individuals, share resources and information, and engage in advocacy and activism online.

By utilizing these resources, individuals within the LGBTQ+ community can find opportunities to get involved in activism and advocacy and make a meaningful impact on the world around them. In the next subchapter, we will explore the future of LGBTQ+ activism and advocacy.

7.5: The Future of LGBTQ+ Activism and Advocacy

The future of LGBTQ+ activism and advocacy is constantly evolving, as new challenges and opportunities arise. Here are some key trends and issues to watch in the coming years:

1.	Intersectionality: Intersectionality, or the recognition of the ways in which different forms of oppression and discrimination intersect, is becoming an increasingly important part of LGBTQ+ activism and advocacy. This may involve working with other marginalized groups, such as people of color, individuals with disabilities, and those from low-income backgrounds, to create more inclusive and equitable spaces and movements.

2.	Transgender Rights: The fight for transgender rights is an increasingly important part of LGBTQ+ activism and advocacy. This may involve advocating for legal protections, raising awareness about transgender issues, and challenging harmful stereotypes and biases.

3.   Global Activism: Activism and advocacy are increasingly taking on a global scope, as LGBTQ+ individuals and allies work to create change in countries around the world. This may involve partnering with international organizations, engaging in online advocacy and campaigns, and supporting local activists and advocates in other countries.

4.   Youth Activism: Youth activism is playing an increasingly important role in LGBTQ+ advocacy and activism, as young people take the lead in creating change and challenging the status quo. This may involve creating and participating in youth-led initiatives, providing support and resources for LGBTQ+ youth, and encouraging young people to get involved in advocacy and activism.

5.   Digital Advocacy: The rise of digital media and online communities has created new opportunities for LGBTQ+ advocacy and activism. This may involve engaging in online campaigns, creating and sharing content on social media, and using digital platforms to connect with other activists and advocates.

By staying informed about these trends and issues, and by continuing to engage in activism and advocacy, individuals within the LGBTQ+ community can help shape the future of the movement and work towards a more just and equitable world for all.

Activism and advocacy have played a critical role in promoting LGBTQ+ rights and creating social change. From the Stonewall riots to the fight for marriage equality, activism and advocacy have been instrumental in securing legal protections, public recognition, and cultural acceptance for the LGBTQ+ community.

Getting involved in activism and advocacy can be a meaningful and empowering way for LGBTQ+ individuals to make a difference in their communities and beyond. By understanding the issues, building connections with others, and creating effective campaigns and initiatives, individuals can work towards a more just and equitable world for all.

By exploring the different types of activism and advocacy, finding the issues and causes that resonate with you, and utilizing the resources available, individuals within the LGBTQ+ community can make a meaningful impact and work towards a more just and equitable world for all.

As we look towards the future of LGBTQ+ activism and advocacy, it is important to recognize the evolving trends and issues that are shaping the movement. By staying informed, engaging in ongoing learning and education, and continuing to fight for change, individuals within the LGBTQ+ community can help shape the future of the movement and create a better world for all.

By working together, supporting one another, and never losing sight of the importance of activism and advocacy, we can continue to empower change and work towards a more just and equitable future for all members of the LGBTQ+ community.

Chapter 8: Resources

As an LGBTQ+ individual, it is important to have access to resources and support to help navigate the challenges and opportunities that arise. From health and wellness to legal and policy issues, education and professional opportunities to community and social connections, there are a variety of resources available to support the needs of LGBTQ+ individuals.

This chapter will provide an overview of some of the key resources that are available to individuals within the LGBTQ+ community, as well as tips for accessing and utilizing these resources effectively. By taking advantage of the resources that are available, individuals can find support, connect with others, and work towards a more just and equitable world for all.

8.1: Health and Wellness Resources

As an LGBTQ+ individual, maintaining physical, mental, and emotional health is an important part of overall well-being. However, navigating the healthcare system and accessing supportive resources can be challenging for many LGBTQ+ individuals. Here are some key health and wellness resources that may be helpful:

1.	LGBTQ+ Healthcare Providers: Finding healthcare providers who are knowledgeable and supportive of LGBTQ+ individuals can be an important part of accessing quality healthcare. Some resources for finding LGBTQ+ healthcare providers include the Gay and Lesbian Medical Association (GLMA) and the Health Professionals Advancing LGBTQ Equality (previously known as the Gay and Lesbian Medical Association).

2.	Support Groups: Support groups can be a helpful way to connect with others who are facing similar challenges and share information and resources. There are a variety of LGBTQ+ support groups available, including those for individuals who are coming out, those who are dealing with mental health issues, and those who are coping with substance use disorders.

3.	Mental Health Resources: Mental health can be a particularly important area of focus for LGBTQ+ individuals, who may face unique challenges related to discrimination and stigma. Some resources for LGBTQ+ mental health include the Trevor Project, which provides crisis intervention and suicide prevention services, and the Association for LGBTQ+ Psychiatrists, which provides resources for finding LGBTQ+ friendly mental health providers.

4.	Online Resources: There are a variety of online resources available to support the health and wellness of LGBTQ+ individuals. These may include informational websites, social media groups and forums, and online mental health resources.

By utilizing these health and wellness resources, individuals within the LGBTQ+ community can find support, access quality healthcare, and maintain physical, mental, and emotional well-being. In the next section, we will explore some of the key legal and policy resources that are available to support the needs of LGBTQ+ individuals.

8.2: Legal and Policy Resources

Legal and policy issues can have a significant impact on the lives of LGBTQ+ individuals, from employment discrimination to hate crimes to access to healthcare. However, navigating the legal system and understanding legal and policy issues can be challenging. Here are some key legal and policy resources that may be helpful:

1.   Advocacy Organizations: There are a variety of advocacy organizations that focus on legal and policy issues affecting the LGBTQ+ community. These organizations work to promote legal protections and advocate for policy change at the local, state, and federal levels. Some examples of advocacy organizations include the Human Rights Campaign (HRC), the National Center for Transgender Equality (NCTE), and the National LGBTQ+ Task Force.

2.	Legal Aid Services: Legal aid services can provide legal assistance and representation to individuals who may not have the financial resources to hire an attorney. These services may be provided through nonprofit organizations or government agencies. Some examples of legal aid services that focus on LGBTQ+ issues include the Lambda Legal Defense and Education Fund and the American Civil Liberties Union (ACLU).

3.	Online Resources: There are a variety of online resources available to help LGBTQ+ individuals understand legal and policy issues and navigate the legal system. These may include informational websites, online legal resources, and advocacy tools for contacting lawmakers and policymakers.

4.	Know Your Rights Workshops: Know Your Rights workshops can be a helpful way to learn about legal and policy issues affecting the LGBTQ+ community and understand your legal rights. These workshops may be offered by advocacy organizations or legal aid services.

By utilizing these legal and policy resources, individuals within the LGBTQ+ community can stay informed about legal issues, access legal assistance and representation, and advocate for policy change. In the next section, we will explore some of the key educational and professional resources that are available to support the needs of LGBTQ+ individuals.

8.3: Educational and Professional Resources

Education and professional opportunities are important components of personal and career growth for LGBTQ+ individuals. However, LGBTQ+ individuals may face unique challenges in accessing educational and professional resources, such as discrimination and bias. Here are some key educational and professional resources that may be helpful:

1.   Scholarships: There are a variety of scholarships available to LGBTQ+ individuals to support educational opportunities, including undergraduate and graduate programs. Some examples of LGBTQ+ scholarships include the Point Foundation Scholarship, the LEAGUE Foundation Scholarship, and the Queer Foundation Scholarships.

2.   Mentorship Programs: Mentorship programs can be a helpful way to connect with professionals in your field who can provide guidance and support. Some examples of LGBTQ+ mentorship programs include the Out for Undergrad Business Conference and the National Organization of Gay and Lesbian Scientists and Technical Professionals (NOGLSTP).

3.   Job Placement Services: Job placement services can help LGBTQ+ individuals connect with job opportunities that are inclusive and supportive. Some examples of job placement services that focus on LGBTQ+ job seekers include Out & Equal CareerLink and the Human Rights Campaign's Corporate Equality Index.

4.	Professional Associations: Professional associations can provide LGBTQ+ individuals with networking opportunities, professional development resources, and access to job opportunities. Some examples of LGBTQ+ professional associations include the National Gay & Lesbian Chamber of Commerce and the National LGBTQ+ Bar Association.

By utilizing these educational and professional resources, LGBTQ+ individuals can access opportunities for personal and career growth, connect with supportive professionals and peers, and find meaningful work opportunities. In the next section, we will explore some of the key community and social resources that are available to support the needs of LGBTQ+ individuals.

8.4: Community and Social Resources

Community and social connections are essential for promoting a sense of belonging and acceptance for LGBTQ+ individuals. However, finding inclusive and supportive community spaces and social opportunities can be challenging. Here are some key community and social resources that may be helpful:

1.	Community Organizations: There are a variety of community organizations that focus on providing support and resources for LGBTQ+ individuals, including advocacy organizations, social clubs, and religious institutions. Some examples of community organizations include the Gay Men's Chorus, PFLAG, and the Metropolitan Community Church.

2.	Support Groups: Support groups can be a helpful way to connect with others who are facing similar challenges and share information and resources. There are a variety of LGBTQ+ support groups available, including those for individuals who are coming out, those who are dealing with mental health issues, and those who are coping with substance use disorders.

3.	LGBTQ+ Social Events: Social events can provide opportunities for LGBTQ+ individuals to connect with one another in a fun and supportive environment. Some examples of LGBTQ+ social events include Pride festivals, LGBTQ+ film festivals, and LGBTQ+ sports leagues.

4.	Online Resources: There are a variety of online resources available to support community and social connections for LGBTQ+ individuals, including social media groups and forums, online chat rooms, and informational websites.

By utilizing these community and social resources, LGBTQ+ individuals can find support, connect with others, and promote a sense of belonging and acceptance. In the next section, we will explore some of the key online resources and tools that are available to support the needs of LGBTQ+ individuals.

In this chapter, we have explored a variety of resources that are available to support the needs of LGBTQ+ individuals, including health and wellness resources, legal and policy resources, educational and professional resources, and community and social resources. By utilizing these resources effectively, LGBTQ+ individuals can find support, access quality healthcare, maintain physical and emotional well-being, and connect with others in meaningful ways.

It is important to remember that resources and support are available, but accessing and utilizing these resources can be challenging. If you are struggling to find the support and resources that you need, consider reaching out to a trusted friend, family member, or mental health professional. You are not alone, and there are people and organizations that are dedicated to supporting the needs of the LGBTQ+ community.

Conclusion

In this guide, we have explored a wide range of topics related to the LGBTQ+ community, including LGBTQ+ identities, coming out, relationships, health and wellness, legal rights, activism, and resources. Our goal has been to provide a comprehensive and inclusive guide that can serve as a valuable resource for individuals who identify as LGBTQ+ or who wish to support the LGBTQ+ community.

As we have explored throughout this guide, the LGBTQ+ community faces many challenges, from discrimination and stigma to lack of access to quality healthcare and legal protections. However, we have also seen that there are many resources and support systems available to help individuals navigate these challenges and promote positive change.

If you are struggling with issues related to your LGBTQ+ identity or wish to get more involved in advocacy and activism, we encourage you to utilize the resources and support systems that we have explored in this guide. Remember that you are not alone, and that there are people and organizations that are dedicated to supporting the needs of the LGBTQ+ community.

Above all, we hope that this guide has served as a valuable resource for individuals who identify as LGBTQ+ or who wish to learn more about the LGBTQ+ community. By promoting understanding, acceptance, and inclusivity, we can work together to create a more supportive and equitable world for all individuals, regardless of their sexual orientation or gender identity.

Call to Action for Supporting the LGBTQ+ Community

Educate yourself and others about LGBTQ+ identities and experiences: It is important to educate yourself and others about LGBTQ+ identities, experiences, and issues. This can involve reading books, articles, and other resources, attending LGBTQ+ events and activities, and engaging in conversations with people from the LGBTQ+ community. By increasing your understanding and knowledge of LGBTQ+ identities and experiences, you can better support and advocate for the community.

Speak out against discrimination and prejudice towards LGBTQ+ individuals: Discrimination and prejudice towards LGBTQ+ individuals can take many forms, from overt acts of violence and hate speech to more subtle forms of discrimination, such as exclusion or microaggressions. It is important to speak out against these behaviors and to support policies and laws that protect the rights of LGBTQ+ individuals.

Advocate for policies and laws that protect the rights of LGBTQ+ individuals: There are many policies and laws that can help to protect the rights of LGBTQ+ individuals, such as anti-discrimination laws, hate crime laws, and marriage equality. By advocating for these policies and laws, you can help to create a more just and equitable society for LGBTQ+ individuals.

Support LGBTQ+ organizations and events: There are many organizations and events that support the LGBTQ+ community, such as LGBTQ+ community centers, pride events, and advocacy groups. By supporting these organizations and events, you can help to create a more supportive and inclusive environment for LGBTQ+ individuals.

Work towards greater understanding and inclusivity within your own community and social circles: You can work towards creating a more inclusive and supportive environment for LGBTQ+ individuals within your own community and social circles. This can involve challenging biases and stereotypes, engaging in conversations about LGBTQ+ issues, and creating opportunities for LGBTQ+ individuals to participate and feel welcomed.

Listen to and elevate the voices of LGBTQ+ individuals, particularly those from marginalized communities: It is important to listen to and elevate the voices of LGBTQ+ individuals, particularly those from marginalized communities. By centering the experiences and perspectives of LGBTQ+ individuals, we can gain a better understanding of the issues and challenges facing the community.

Challenge your own biases and privilege, and work towards being an ally and advocate for the LGBTQ+ community: We all have biases and privileges that can impact our interactions with LGBTQ+ individuals. It is important to challenge these biases and privileges and to work towards being an ally and advocate for the LGBTQ+ community. This can involve self-reflection, education, and taking action to support and uplift the voices of LGBTQ+ individuals.

Supporting the LGBTQ+ community involves recognizing and respecting the diversity of gender and sexual identities, as well as the intersecting identities that shape a person's experiences and opportunities. It requires a commitment to challenging discrimination and prejudice, advocating for policies and laws that protect the rights of LGBTQ+ individuals, and working towards greater understanding and inclusivity within our own communities and social circles.

By taking action to support the LGBTQ+ community, we can help to create a more just and equitable society where all individuals, regardless of their gender or sexual identity, are treated with respect, dignity, and equality. Let us strive to be allies and advocates for the LGBTQ+ community, and work towards creating a world where everyone can live and thrive free from discrimination and oppression.